A Kodansha Comics Trade Paperback Original
Blue Period 12 copyright © 2022 Tsubasa Yamaguchi
English translation copyright © 2023 Tsubasa Yamaguchi

Published in the United States by Kodansha Comics, an imprint of Kodansha USA Publishing, LLC, New York.

Publication rights for this English edition arranged through Kodansha Ltd., Tokyo.

First published in Japan in 2022 by Kodansha Ltd., Tokyo.

ISBN 978-1-64651-567-7

Printed in the United States of America.

www.kodansha.us

9 8 7 6 5 4 3 2 1
Translation: Ajani Oloye
Lettering: Lys Blakeslee
Editing: Haruko Hashimoto
Kodansha Comics edition cover design by Matthew Akuginow

Publisher: Kiichiro Sugawara

Director of publishing services: Ben Applegate
Director of publishing operations: Dave Barrett
Associate director of publishing operations: Stephen Pakula
Publishing services managing editors: Madison Salters, Alanna Ruse, with Grace Chen
Production manager: Emi Lotto
Logo and character art ©Kodansha USA Publishing, LLC

A PROSPEROUS EIGHT,

AND A BOLD AND DARING TIGER.

THOUGH, THE TIGER IN *THE MOON OVER THE MOUNTAIN* WAS PORTRAYED AS A MONSTER OF PRIDE...

The Moon Over the Mountain, page 105

The Moon Over the Mountain (also known as *Tiger-Poet* and, in Japanese, *Sangetsuki*) is a short story by Atsushi Nakajima. Like many of his works, this story was based on a Classical Chinese story from the Tang Dynasty. The story is about a civil servant named Li Zheng whose monstrous pride turns him into a tiger. He passes the civil servant exams and is able to do well in his job, but feels the job is beneath him and quits to pursue his true passion, poetry. Unfortunately, he can't make ends meet as a poet, and he returns to his civil servant job, taking a lower position than before. This badly hurts his pride and drives him mad, eventually turning him into a tiger that still retains his human mind but is unable to write, which is a hellish existence for Li Zheng.

The sacred and secular, page 182

Hare and *ke* is a concept of dual temporalities most often used in Japanese folklore studies. Though there are several interpretations, *hare* can refer to "good weather," or a positive turn in the weather, and are sacred days of celebration, ritual, festival, change—essentially, they are extraordinary days. Special

WOULD IT MAKE MORE SENSE TO YOU IF...I SAID IT WAS AS DIFFICULT AS TEACHING FOREIGNERS TO GET A FEEL FOR JAPANESE CULTURE, SUCH AS THE CONCEPT OF *THE SACRED AND SECULAR* OR *KEIGO* FORMAL SPEECH?

attire, dishes, manners, and access to sacred locations may be associated with *hare*. On the other hand, *ke*, which is thought to refer to "qi" or "food," represents ordinary daily life. These distinctions can be fluid and have changed over time.

TRANSLATION NOTES

Ketchup spaghetti, page 21

The dish that Professor Inukai dislikes is actually known as *Napolitan* (or *Naporitan*), a Western-influenced pasta dish made with ketchup in place of the standard tomato sauce. Additional ingredients include bell peppers, onions, button mushrooms, Japanese-style sausage, or bacon (typically processed, pre-cooked, and with a ham-like texture). Cafés and restaurants that serve *Napolitan* typically boil the pasta, let it rest, and then reheat it with the other ingredients before being served.

The origin of this dish is unclear, but many people believe it was invented in the 1950s in Yokohama at the New Grand Hotel. And despite a name derived from the Italian city of Naples, *Napolitan* is said to have been inspired by dishes American soldiers would eat during the occupation of Japan.

Washi paper, page 30

Washi, also known as Japanese paper (and often mistakenly referred to as "rice paper"), is a traditional paper made from plant fibers. Most washi paper is made from mulberry (*kozo*) bark, but other varieties are made from the bark of the Edgeworth chrysantha (*mitsumata*) bush or *ganpi* shrub.

OGI-SAN AND HAMAKI-SAN ARE A COUPLE.

EVERY MORNING, THEY TAKE A 30-MINUTE WALK TOGETHER.

THEY HELP EACH OTHER OUT WITH WORK.

THEY ALSO WATCH COMEDY VIDEOS TOGETHER BEFORE GOING TO SLEEP.

NASU-SAN'S...

...BEST DISH IS CURRY.

SO MUCH SO THAT HE GOES TO INDIA TO GET HIS SPICES.

HE GOES TO NEPAL TO UNDERSTAND NAAN BREAD.

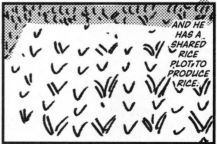

AND HE HAS A SHARED RICE PLOT TO PRODUCE RICE.

THE MEMBERS OF NO MARKs (1)

THE LEADER OF NO MARKs

He's got that intense battle-manga drive...

Blue Period was created with the support of many people!

Special Thanks

Thank you so very much!

Meguru Yamaguchi-sama
Thank you for collaborating with me on the anime in addition to everything else! Please allow me to join you for a meal when I go to America someday!

Makoto Aida-sama
Thank you for letting me borrow your precious piece...! I've been hoping to have something of yours in my manga ever since the talk we did before, so I'm so glad this could happen.

Tamana Moteki-sama
I'm always grateful to you! You continue to contribute such awesome paintings. Your landscapes are one thing, but I also love your paintings of people, Tamana-chan... Thank you very much! Let's keep doing this!

Ikuo Masumoto-sama
Thank you so much for responding so willingly despite a request that was so close to the deadline. Please allow me to see you in person sometime...!

Research Cooperation: Thank you so much to Yoichi Umetsu-sama, and Shinjuku Ophthalmologist (Ganka) Gallery!

We'll be holding a *Blue Period* exhibition!

The stage play was also awesome!

YEAH, ABOUT THAT...

WHAT WE TALKED ABOUT ON THE TRAIN THE OTHER DAY...

SO, BEFORE...

OH.

HISA-YAMA-SAN!

ピ九...
PAUSE

I'M NEVER COMING BACK HERE AGAIN...

COULD I GET YOUR OPINION ON MY NEXT ASSIGNMENT?

SHE'S AMAZING.

WHEN I TALK TO HER...

OF COURSE!

NOW...

NOW, OF ALL TIMES...

IS THERE A POINT TO DOING THIS AS A PAINTING?

SOME-THING SO SIMPLE...

...

AND DESPITE HOW LOW-LEVEL I AM...

SHE TOOK SOMETHING DIFFICULT AND SIMPLIFIED IT FOR ME.

NO, THAT'S NOT RIGHT.

UM...

...FUJI-SAN MADE WHAT SHE WAS SAYING UNDER-STANDABLE AND ENGAGED IN CONVERSATION WITHOUT MAKING FUN OF ME.

YOU CAN'T EXCLUDE PEOPLE WHO DON'T KNOW ABOUT THESE THINGS.

YOU'RE LEARNING THIS NOW? THIS STUFF IS ART 101.

ART IS SUPPOSED TO REACH ACROSS ALL BORDERS TO ENRICH THE LIVES OF PEOPLE, AND YET THERE ARE PEOPLE WHO DON'T UNDERSTAND THAT.

AND I BELIEVE THAT LACK OF UNDERSTANDING IS A PRETTY NATURAL WAY OF THINKING.

SO, IN ADDITION TO WESTERN CULTURE, RELIGIONS SUCH AS CHRISTIANITY AND JUDAISM, AS WELL AS GENERAL WESTERN HISTORY, ARE ALSO BROADLY ASSOCIATED WITH WESTERN ART HISTORY.

THAT'S WHY IT CAN BE HARD FOR JAPANESE PEOPLE TO FEEL FAMILIAR WITH WESTERN "ART."

...BUT IS RELIGION REALLY THAT IMPORTANT?

LEONARDO DAVINCI, *THE LAST SUPPER*

...!

WOULD IT MAKE MORE SENSE TO YOU IF...I SAID IT WAS AS DIFFICULT AS TEACHING FOREIGNERS TO GET A FEEL FOR JAPANESE CULTURE, SUCH AS THE CONCEPT OF *THE SACRED AND SECULAR* OR *KEIGO* FORMAL SPEECH?

HMM...

BUT THAT'S LIMITED TO THE HISTORY OF *FINE ART IN JAPAN.*

THERE SURE IS.

WAIT...HUH? WHAT'RE YOU SAYING? I MEAN, THERE'S ART IN JAPAN, TOO...

FINE-ART HISTORY EXISTS IN JAPAN, AFRICA, AS WELL AS RUSSIA.

HOW-EVER...

KATSUSHIKA HOKUSAI, *THIRTY-SIX VIEWS OF MOUNT FUJI, THE KAZUSA PROVINCE SEA ROUTE*

SIMON DE MYLE, *NOAH'S ARK ON MOUNT ARARAT*

...AND THIS ARK TREATS THE HISTORY OF FINE ART IN EUROPE, OR WHAT PEOPLE CALL "WESTERN ART HISTORY," AS THE "OFFICIAL" HISTORY OF ART.

THE IDEA OF "ART" IS A GARGANTUAN ARK THAT CONTAINS EVERY TYPE OF FINE ART...

...UM, BUT, AS EMBARRASSING AS THIS IS TO ADMIT, THERE WERE A LOT OF PARTS THAT I DIDN'T UNDERSTAND...

NO, THANK YOU VERY MUCH. REALLY.

OH, THAT'S FANTASTIC.

SMIIIILE

OHH, YES...

YOU'RE RIGHT ABOUT THAT.

WHAT KIND OF PARTS?

"ART" COMES FROM WESTERN CULTURE, AFTER ALL.

HUH?

UHH, WELL...

THERE'S A LOT OF BACK-GROUND INFO I NEEDED TO KNOW, AND THERE WERE PLENTY OF FOREIGN TERMS AND NAMES...

THOSE ARE SOME HUGE SLUGS YOU GOT THERE, YATORA-KUN!

Under your eyes.

GLOOOM...

OH, WOOOW!

← Bags under his eyes

OH MY!

ALSO, I'VE GONE TO A BUNCH OF DIFFERENT SHOWS LATELY...

I WANTED TO STOP BY SINCE I FINISHED READING THE BOOK I BORROWED...

...

YOU'RE A QUICK READER.

NOT REALLY... IT WAS INTERESTING, SO I JUST...

DID HE REALLY NEED TO ASK ABOUT HIS SCHOOLING??!!

IS GOING TO UNIVERSITY SUCH AN IMPORTANT THING?

I MEAN, THEY LET ME INTO ONE, BUT...

REALLY? ISN'T IT ENOUGH AS LONG AS HIS PIECES ARE GOOD?

WHERE HE WENT TO SCHOOL HAS NOTHING TO DO WITH HIS WORK, RIGHT?

...

I'M HOME, AND YEAH, IT'S BEEN A WHILE...

YAKKUN, WELCOME BACK!

OH, HEY, BEEN A WHILE, YATORAAA...

BETCHA 100 YEN HE WAS STAYING AT HIS GIRLFRIEND'S PLACE.

The Story of Art

OH, IS THAT SO?

I'M SELF-TAUGHT...

OHH... I HAVEN'T GONE TO ANY ART SCHOOL.

THAT'S WHAT I THOUGHT.

...WAIT, HAS HE NOT NOTICED ME? MAYBE HE DOESN'T REMEMBER ME?

BUT MAYBE HE'S A LITTLE DIFFERENT THAN I WAS IMAGINING HIM TO BE...

YAKUMO-SAN SAID HE WAS THE MOST DISTINGUISHED PROFESSOR IN OIL PAINTING,

SO HE GOES TO SHOWS FOR YOUNG ARTISTS...?

OH, YES...

TELL ME...

WHICH ART UNIVERSITY DID YOU GRADUATE FROM?

ART: IKUO MASUMOTO

I...CAME HERE ON IMPULSE...

OKAY.

PLEASE WRITE YOUR NAME DOWN HERE.

CHATTER

CHATTER

IS THIS OKAY? THEY'RE NOT GOING TO MAKE ME BUY SOMETHING, ARE THEY?

AND IT KIND OF SEEMS LIKE EVERYONE KNOWS EACH OTHER HERE...

...BUT IT'S HARD TO GO INTO A SINGLE ROOM IN A MULTI-TENANT BUILDING...!

IF SOMEONE
COULD CHOOSE
MY ENTIRE LIFE
FOR ME...

...FEEL BAD ABOUT BEING LEFT BEHIND.

"I DON'T WANT TO FEEL LIKE I'VE WASTED FOUR YEARS OF MY LIFE."

BUT I DON'T HAVE IT IN ME TO QUIT SCHOOL JUST YET.

...University of the Arts
...Year Oil Painting Concentratio...

...I THOUGHT THE PERSON WHO MADE THIS ART IS THE TYPE WHO WOULD GAIN MORE FROM REAL AND CONCRETE EXPERIENCE THAN THE ABSTRACT REVIEWS YOU GET IN ART SCHOOL.

...duce a piece based on ...he theme of "guilt"

HOW LONG ARE YOU GOING TO KEEP DOING THE SAME THING?

BECAUSE I CAN STILL GO TO NO MARKs EVEN IF I CONTINUE GOING TO UNIVERSITY.

I DON'T EXACTLY...

...l not be accepted.
...nt of your pieces on th...

OKAMOTO-KUN, YOTASUKE-KUN...

OH, SO THAT'S WHAT'S HAPPEN-ING...!

...

THANK GOODNESS. I WAS SUR-PRISED TO SEE ALL THIS WHEN WE STILL HAVE MORE THAN A MONTH TO GO.

AH HA HA!

YEAAAH, EVEN THOUGH IT HAS NOTHING TO DO WITH MY OWN!

DOESN'T SEEING EVERY-ONE ELSE'S PROGRESS MAKE YOU ANXIOUSSS?

"YAGUCHI-KUN, IF YOU'RE CONSIDERING THE SAME THING, YOU SHOULD MAKE A DECISION SOONER RATHER THAN LATER."

Art

based on guilt

I GUESS I COULD AT LEAST FIGURE OUT THE FORMAT.

Haaah...

OH, YAGUCHI-KUN!

MAN, EVERYONE'S PRETTY FAR ALONG WITH THEIR PIECES...

Hüllo!

IT'S BEEN A WHILE!

IT'S AMAZING HOW THE PEOPLE WITH LARGE PIECES HAVE MADE SO MUCH PROGRESS, HUH.

EUGH.

...BUT AFTER SEEING NO MARKS, I THOUGHT I SHOULD BE GETTING INTO THE REAL ART WORLD SOONER THAN LATER.

AH HA HA. YOU'RE THE FIRST PERSON I'VE TOLD.

I'M NOT LEARNING ANYTHING FROM ART SCHOOL ANYWAY.

YAGUCHI-KUN...

...IF YOU'RE CONSIDERING THE SAME THING, YOU SHOULD MAKE A DECISION SOONER RATHER THAN LATER.

ART SCHOOL'S A WASTE OF TIME. PLUS, IF I DON'T HAVE TO GO TO SCHOOL, I COULD SAVE THE MONEY I WOULD USE ON TUITION *AND* WORK PART-TIME.

BEFORE GETTING INTO TUA, I FAILED AND RETOOK THE ENTRANCE EXAM MORE THAN ONCE, AND I REALLY WORKED MY ASS OFF TO GET HERE...

BUILDING: TOKYO UNIVERSITY OF THE ARTS

I DON'T WANT TO FEEL LIKE I'VE WASTED FOUR YEARS OF MY LIFE.

I DIDN'T THINK YOU'D BE THIS INTO NO MARKS, YAGUCHI-KUN.

HUH?

OH... OH, YEAH...

KTNK ゴト.....

KTHNK ゴト.....

THEY HAVE ALL THOSE ART BOOKS... PLUS, EVERYONE'S SO NICE.

Wha?!

I THINK I'M GOING TO SUBMIT A NOTICE OF WITHDRAWAL NEXT WEEK...

AND THEY HAVE PEOPLE THERE WHO ARE SERIOUSLY MAKING ART WITHOUT HAVING TO GO TO ART SCHOOL...

YEAH.

YOU KNOW...

...

...AND BEING LIKE THAT, SHE'S AN ABSOLUTE GENIUS AT TUNING THE HEARTS AND MINDS OF OTHERS...

...WITHOUT EVER HAVING TO BEND HER OWN OPINIONS.

THAT'S HOW YOU MAKE ENEMIES, YOU KNOW.

TAKADA-KUUUN.

Scary...

SHUT UP!

...THAT THIS PER-SON...

BUT YOU MAKE ART THAT PLACES A HEAVY EMPHASIS ON THE CONCEPT.

UH...

YOU END UP STARTLING PEOPLE WHEN YOU FLASH YOUR DAGGER AT OTHERS LIKE THAT.

RIGHT?

...IS SMART...

...AND TAKES THINGS AT HER OWN PACE.

AFTER TWO WEEKS HERE, I UNDER-STOOD...

GLANCE

Art

BUT MOST OFTEN...

...AND OTHERS DO THINGS STREAMERS WOULD, LIKE MAKING BUCKET FLAN OR PUTTING MENTOS INTO COLA.

AT NO MARKs, EVERYONE BASICALLY SLEEPS ON THE FLOOR IN THE SAME SPACE.

SOME OF THE PEOPLE HERE PRODUCE ART...

AND HERE IS TODAY'S WORK OF ART!

UGHH! WHY IS JAPANESE TV LIKE THIS?!

THEY ONLY EVER INTRODUCE PEOPLE TO *REALISTIC ART* OF *LANDSCAPES AND LIVING* THINGS MADE WITH *COMMON MATERIALS!*

Hiru Hiru!
Genius Art

Looks just like the real thing

Took about a month to complete

Made with 12,000 matches!!

IT TOOK ABOUT A MONTH TO COMPLETE!

MATCHSTICK ART THAT LOOKS EXACTLY LIKE A REAL KITTY CAT!

IT WAS MADE WITH 12,000 MATCHES.

KIRIO FUJI.

NO MARKs' LEADER. SHE'S WEIRD, BUT SHE'S AN ALL-AROUND KNOWLEDGE-ABLE PERSON, AND SHE'S CHARISMATIC.

WAH...!

WOW!

WAAAAAAH!

AND THE SHARE HOUSE VIBE HERE AT NO MARKs' ISN'T REALLY MY THING...

AT FIRST, I JUST CAME HERE TO HELP OUT.

AND MORE THAN ANY-THING ELSE...

SHRRR

...BUT THEY HAVE TONS OF ART BOOKS AND REFERENCE MATERIAL.

I HAVEN'T GONE TO SCHOOL ONCE IN OVER TWO WEEKS.

HEY, COME HERE, EVERY-ONE!

THE SNAILS ARE MATING!

YOUR PROFESSOR JUST... *SKIPPED* YOUR REVIEW?!

WHAT...?!

I'D BE DEMANDING THAT HE DO THE REVIEW, ESPECIALLY AFTER KNOWING HOW MUCH THOSE PROFESSORS ARE PAID!

GUHHH! THAT'S AWFUL! THE WORST!

IT HAPPENED IN MY FIRST YEAR.

...

WELL, I GUESS IT'S GOOD YOU WERE SPARED FROM WHATEVER BULLSHIT THAT WOULD'VE COME YOUR WAY!

THAT SOUNDS ROUGH...

STROKE 52

WHEN THE GROUND SOFTENS, YOU QUICKLY GET STUCK

BLUE PERIOD

For eggplant curry,
grill the eggplants
and include miso as a
secret ingredient.

YEAH.

I NEVER KNEW THEY HAD A PLACE LIKE THAT IN AKIHABARA!

THAT OWL CAFÉ WAS GREAT! THE OWLS WERE SO CUTE!

I HAVEN'T SEEN HIM IN SCHOOL LATELY...

YAGUCHI-SAN...

NO, THERE WERE MORE THAN THAT.

Hmmm...

I GO TO AROUND 200 SHOWS PER YEAR...

55 PEOPLE ...?

I GUESS... I DIDN'T EXPECT I'D LEAVE AN IMPRESSION OUT OF THE 55 PEOPLE ON DISPLAY THERE...

I'M SERIOUSLY *SO* HAPPY RIGHT NOW!

...AND YOURS WAS ONE OF THE PIECES I REMEMBERED.

BUILDING: TOKYO UNIVERSITY OF THE ARTS

WAUGHH! SO CUUUTE!

WHAT A CUTE OWL!

HOO HOOO!

I REMEMBER SENSING THAT WHOEVER MADE THIS MUST REALLY BE STRUGGLING WITH SELF-DOUBT.

THAT'S THE FEEL I GOT WHEN I SAW IT.

I CAN'T JUDGE YOU COMPLETELY OFF OF THIS ONE PAINTING...

...BUT I FEEL THAT YOU VALUE THINGS THAT RELATE TO PEOPLE...

THE PAINTING TOLD ME THE ARTIST WAS CLEVER, BUT NOT A FULLY LOGICAL TYPE— ALMOST LIKE AN ATHLETE IN THE WAY THEY MIGHT FORCE THEIR BODY TO LEARN FROM PRODUCING PIECE AFTER PIECE AFTER PIECE.

BUT STILL, THE PAINTING FELT COMPACT, AND WAS RELYING ON TECHNIQUE...

YEAH... IT REMINDS ME OF EMIL NOLDÉ OR DE KOONING. AT THE SURFACE LEVEL, IT COULD ALMOST BE A TRACING OF THEIR WORK.

...AND I THOUGHT THE PERSON WHO MADE THIS ART...

HERE. TAKE A LOOK...

YATORA-KUN.

TAP

TAP

TAP

TAP

...!!

I MEAN, THIS IS FROM LAST YEAR'S END-OF-YEAR SHOW FOR FIRST-YEAR OIL PAINTING, RIGHT?

HUH?

SO, THIS WAS YOU.

WOW, I SEE NOW...

I WAS THERE, SINCE THE REVIEWS WERE OPEN TO THE PUBLIC.

Waugh! It feels like I'm doing something bad...

IT'S BREEZY.

AHHH, UM...

THIS IS THE FIRST TIME I'VE SEEN A GIRL WITH AN UNDER-CU...

ZHRF

EHH...

HUH?

WHA?

THAT REMINDS ME, I HEARD THIS FROM KISARAGI-SAN, BUT...

...YATORA-SAN, YOU'RE A TUA STUDENT, RIGHT?

OHH, YEAH. ACTUALLY, I DO HAVE SOME...

BUT I'M REALLY NO GOOD. I'M NOT SO SURE THAT I CAN EVEN CALL MYSELF AN ART STUDENT...

YAAAY!

OH, BUT YOU SAID YOU DON'T HAVE PICS ON YOU.

I'D LIKE TO SEE YOUR WORK.

...YEAH.

VUM
VUM

Oh, yeah, that...

BA-BMP

FUJI-SAN.

YEAH.

Hyaaah!

...ABOUT THE CONVERSATION WE HAD THE OTHER DAY.

WANNA TOUCH IT?

Y-YOU HAVE AN UNDER-CUT...?!

FLUP

THE OTHER DAY?

Mm.

...ククククA

SHF

GUESS I'LL FINISH THIS CURRY AND HEAD HOME...

EVEN IF I JUST WANTED TO SAY HELLO TO FUJI-SAN, IT WOULD BE IMPOSSIBLE IN A SITUATION LIKE THIS...

BOTH KISARAGI-SAN AND HISAYAMA-SAN WENT OFF TO MAKE "CONNECTIONS."

This curry is so good.

THIS IS SO GOOD! I JUST CAN'T GET ENOUGH OF THIS TASTE, NO MATTER HOW MANY TIMES I'VE HAD IT.

MMMM!

Wait.

What?

CLAMOR CLAMOR

BUT YOU'RE THE ORGA-NIZER...

YEAH, BUT WE'RE OUTSIDE... YOU DON'T NEED TO GO BACK INSIDE?

BATH-ROOM BREAK.

WAIT, DID YOU WARP HERE?!

I'VE AL-WAYS HAD SENSITIVE HEARING.

I'M NOT GOOD WITH THAT STUFF.

BUT IT'S THE KIND OF DREAM I'D TOTALLY FORGET ONCE I WOKE UP.

BUT IT'S SURPRISING HOW I GET CALMER WHEN THE PARTY GETS WILDER...

OMF.

Maybe that's my problem...

*SEE CHAPTER 1.

I'M PROBABLY GONNA FEEL DEAD AFTER THIS...

...I KNOW IF I REALLY HAD FUN DEPENDING ON WHETHER I FEEL DEAD INSIDE THE NEXT DAY.

WITH DRINKING PARTIES...

OH, MAN. PEOPLE AREN'T FORMING A LINE OR ANYTHING, BUT THEY'RE KEEPING THEIR DISTANCE AND WAITING FOR A CHANCE TO TALK TO HER...

I'D EXPECT AS MUCH FROM SOMEONE AS POPULAR AS HER.

THAT REMINDS ME, WHERE'S FUJI-SAN?

SHE'S OVER THERE TALKING TO SOME ACTOR.

OH, SURE...

I DON'T HAVE PICS ON ME NOW, SO IT'LL HAVE TO BE NEXT TIME...

...

EVERYONE IS SO NICE.

AND I'VE EVEN BEEN ABLE TO TALK TO SOME PRETTY AMAZING PEOPLE.

WOW.

THE ATMO-SPHERE IS DAZZLING.

HER FACE IS SO SMALL AND CUTE!

WAIT, ISN'T THAT STICKY SAEKO, THE "MASKING TAPE GIRL"?!

WHO KNEW THAT ART CRITIC MATSUNO-SAN CAME TO THESE THINGS...?!

WHOA! IT'S DJ COLLAGE-MAN!

...I FEEL LIKE MY EXISTENCE BECOMES... UNCOMPLICATED.

...BUT WHEN I TALK TO THIS PERSON...

BUILDING: TOKYO UNIVERSITY OF THE ARTS

GLOO

OOM

THE... FUNCTION OF ART, HUH?

I NEVER THOUGHT OF THAT BEFORE.

SO, TO RETURN TO YOUR FIRST QUESTION,

THAT'S WHY WE'RE DOING THE SHOW AND PARTY TOGETHER.

...OR CONCERNED WITH TECHNIQUES AND THINGS.

I WAS FOCUSED ON HOW GOOD THE CONCEPT WAS...

UP UNTIL NOW,

ART DOESN'T JUST EXIST ON ITS OWN...

...IT EXISTS ON TOP OF HUMAN HISTORY. I GUESS IT'S OBVIOUS...

THAT'S ALL I REALLY CONSIDERED.

BUT I SEE NOW...

I DON'T WANT ART TO BE SOME-THING WE *APPRECIATE.*

I WANT IT TO BE AN IMPORTANT PART OF OUR EVERYDAY LIVES.

ART SHOULDN'T BE GREAT BECAUSE SOMEONE GREAT MADE IT.

BECAUSE ART...

...SHOULDN'T BE A PRIVILEGE ONLY GRANTED TO THE ELITE, NOW, SHOULD IT?

"FINE ART" WAS VERY VALUABLE AS MEDIA AT TIMES WHEN THERE WERE FEW PEOPLE WHO COULD READ.

BUT THESE DAYS, NOT ONLY CAN EVERYONE READ, WE EVEN HAVE TOOLS LIKE "CAMERAS" THAT CAN RECORD THINGS EXACTLY AS WE SEE THEM.

METOBE

SMILE SMILE

OH...

I SEE...

AND SO WE NOW HAVE NEW MEDIA AND FORMS OF EXPRESSION THAT CAN ONLY BE PRODUCED IN OUR MODERN AGE.

AND THOSE THINGS DON'T BELONG TO ROYALTY AND PEOPLE OF INFLUENCE, THEY'RE CLOSE AT HAND TO YOU AND ME.

I APPRECIATE THAT THEY ALLOW US TO VIEW ART THAT YOU USED TO ONLY BE ABLE TO SEE IN ROYAL PALACES, OR PIECES THAT WOULD NORMALLY COST HUNDREDS OF MILLIONS OF YEN, BUT...

AS FAR AS MUSEUMS GO...

OH, YEAH... YOU'RE RIGHT.

JEEZ, GUESS WE'RE STARTING FROM THERE!

UH...

...COULD YOU GIVE ME SOME EXAMPLES OF WHAT YOU MEANT BY **PROPER CONDITIONS** AND **PROPER FUNCTIONS** FOR WORKS OF FINE ART?

...EXCUSE ME, BUT...

WHICH IS BECAUSE MUSEUMS EXIST AS PLACES THAT PRESERVE WORKS OF FINE ART AS CULTURAL ARTIFACTS.

A MUSEUM IS SUITED FOR TAKING YOUR TIME TO FACE AND CAREFULLY EXAMINE WORKS OF ART.

THIS IS MY PERSONAL VIEW, BUT...

FWUP

SURE!

IN THE STORYBOOK OF HISTORY, WORKS OF ART SERVE AS THE ILLUSTRATIONS.

THAT'S WHY ART HISTORY BECOMES EVEN MORE INTERESTING WHEN YOU READ UP ON HISTORY.

THE THING IS, YATORA-KUN...

...WHETHER IT'S A PAIR OF GLASSES, SOME WALLPAPER, OR A PAINTING YOU GOT FROM A FRIEND...

...PUTTING OBJECTS ON DISPLAY IN A PURE-WHITE SPACE TO MARK THEM AS *THINGS TO BE APPRECIATED* IS WEIRD, ISN'T IT?

AND YET... AN ART WORK UNINTENTIONALLY BECOMES THIS... *"THING" TO BE APPRECIATED* SIMPLY BY BEING PLACED IN THOSE... "ART" MUSEUMS.

I FIND THAT TO BE A BIT UNSETTLING.

AN ART WORK SERVES ITS *PROPER FUNCTION* PRECISELY WHEN IT IS PLACED IN ITS *PROPER CONDITIONS.*

IT'S KINDA DIFFERENT FROM THE TYPE OF THING YOU'D SEE IN A MUSEUM.

SO ARE PEOPLE GOING TO DRINK AND PARTY IN FRONT OF THE PIECES?

SPEAKING OF, IT'S PRETTY COOL THAT YOU HAVE A DJ BOOTH IN THE EXHIBITION SPACE.

IF THAT MAKES US LOOK LIKE A CULT, THEN SO BE IT.

SO SHE'S AWARE OF IT.

DO YOU LIKE THEM, YATORA-KUN?

DON'T YOU THINK IT'S DIFFICULT TO UNDERSTAND THINGS WHEN YOU'RE LOOKING AT PIECES IN A MUSEUM?

HUH?

KWIP

KWIP

YES.

MUSEUMS ARE A LITTLE ANNOYING TO ME.

I...

...ACTU-ALLY THINK THAT'S NORMAL.

I...

...GUESS I HAVE THOUGHT THAT, BUT IT WAS WHEN I WAS IN HIGH SCHOOL...

WE CALL THEM "GIFTS" HERE.

A GOOD AMOUNT OF THEM ARE THINGS PEOPLE BROUGHT TO US.

THEY HAVE A HUGE AMOUNT OF ART BOOKS, THOUGH...

ARE ALL OF THESE YOURS, FUJI-SAN?

G-GIFTS?

THAT'S OUR RULE.

KWIP

KWIP

Your gift to us was your labor, Yatora-kun.

IN EXCHANGE, WE ONLY ASK THAT YOU LEAVE ONE THING BEHIND.

AT NO MARKS, ANYONE IS FREE TO COME AND GO, AND STAY THE NIGHT AS THEY PLEASE.

...SO INSTEAD OF MONEY, WE ACCEPT LOVE AND KINDNESS... WE BANK ON PEOPLE'S DESIRES AND GOALS, AND END UP BUILDING RELATIONSHIPS THAT WAY.

NO MARKS ISN'T A BUSI- NESS...

YOU JUST THOUGHT THIS PLACE SEEMS LIKE A CULT, RIGHT?

I DON'T KNOW... SEEMS LIKE A CULT...

YOU'RE UP EARLY, YATORA-KUN.

...OH!

GUH MOHIN...

S-S-S-S-S-Sorry!!

FWUP

Mm...

BACON! BACON'S GREAT...

BACON

BACON

YOU'RE FREE TO READ ANY BOOK OVER THERE.

BUT IF I'M BEING HONEST, SHE DOESN'T SEEM AS INCREDIBLE AS THEY MAKE HER OUT TO BE...

BWOMF

KIRIO FUJI...

Fwaaah...

IT SEEMS LIKE BOTH HISAYAMA-SAN AND KISARAGI-SAN PUT A HUGE AMOUNT OF TRUST IN HER.

...

DO...

DO YOU LIKE MAGENDER?

HERE'S A CHANGE OF CLOTHES.

GO AHEAD AND PUT YOUR USED TOWEL INTO THE WASHING MACHINE.

THAT SMARTPHONE CASE...

I'VE BEEN WONDERING ABOUT THIS FOR A BIT, BUT...

UM, SO...

HER PRICKLY PERSONALITY IS A LITTLE INTIMIDATING...

TAKADA-SAN, WAS IT...?

OKAY...

MAGENDER/WO-SAKANA

OHH MAN! I GET *EXACTLY* WHAT YOU'RE SAYING!!

BUT THE BACK-AND-FORTH BETWEEN KENTO AND HARUTO IS JUST SO INTENSE.

PEOPLE SAY MAGENDER WAS MEANT TO TARGET FEMALE VIEWERS,

I GOT INTO THE DIVER SERIES FROM KOGA, THOUGH.

TAKADA-SAN, DO YOU WATCH MAGENDER...?

HUH?

OH.

LAST WEEK'S EPISODE WAS A MASTERPIECE!

WOULD YOU LIKE TO TAKE A BATH FIRST?

...

SORRY, BUT THE CLOCK HERE IS 10 MINUTES LATE...

0:35

GUESS I'M STAYING THE NIGHT...

WHEN'S MY FIRST CLASS TOMORROW? UGH, I'M SO TIRED...

PHEWW...

OH!

CREAK

SORRY TO USE THE BATH FIRST.

GAH! HOLY CRAP, IT'S ALREADY PAST MIDNIGHT!

HWAAH! I'M POOPED!

HUH?

YATORA-KUN, ARE YOU OKAY TO MAKE THE LAST TRAIN?

I SHOULD ALSO GET GOING...

MAN, MY BACK HURTS! MY BODY'S ACHY AFTER BEING INACTIVE FOR SO LONG.

THANKS! SEE YOU IN TWO DAYS!

GOOD WORK, EVERY-ONE!

HUP

"NO MARKS" IS A PLACE WHERE ANYONE CAN FREELY ENTER AND LEAVE.

ALSO, THIS ISN'T LIMITED TO ART, BUT YOU ALSO ENCOUNTER ADVANTAGES AND DISADVANTAGES BASED ON RACE, GENDER, AND YOUR FINANCIAL SITUATION.

AND EVEN IF YOU GET INTERNET OUT THERE, YOU DON'T HAVE ANYONE AROUND YOU WHO'S IN THE KNOW...

IT DOESN'T MATTER IF YOU'RE POOR OR A DROPOUT, THEY WELCOME ANYONE AS LONG AS YOU LIKE ART. THAT'S THEIR STYLE.

WHOOA! AWESOME!

RIGHT?

AND I HEARD THEIR LEADER KIRIO FUJI HAS PERFECT MEMORY. SHE CAN RECALL ANY BOOK SHE'S READ ONCE, WORD-FOR-WORD.

WOW, THEY'RE SO GENEROUS.

IT'S THE KIND OF PLACE THAT WOULD LOOK PRETTY DAMN APPEALING...

...TO SOMEONE WHO'S GETTING FED UP WITH UNIVERSITY.

"NO MARKS" IS AN ANTI-AUTHORITARIAN ART COLLECTIVE.

...

YAKUMOOO! SO THE TAKARAZUKA KINEN*... WAIT, WHAT?

"NUMB ARSE"? THAT'S SOME POTTY MOUTH Y'GOT THERE, HACCHAN...

WOW, "NO MARKS" GOT THEIR OWN FEATURE.

IN THEIR CASE, THE AUTHORITIES ARE THE RICH, POLITICIANS, AND ART UNIVERSITIES LIKE TUA.

ANTI... AUTHOR... I...TARIAN?

THE WORLD OUTSIDE OF THE CITY IS LIKE A BLACK BOX, CUT OFF FROM INFORMATION.

YOU NEED MONEY TO GET INTO TUA.

PRIVATE SCHOOLS COST TWO MILLION YEN A YEAR, AND JUST GOING TO A PREP SCHOOL ALONE COSTS AT LEAST 300,000 YEN A YEAR.

*A FAMOUS HORSE RACE HELD IN THE CITY OF TAKARAZUKA IN HYOGO PREFECTURE, JAPAN.

AN ART COLLECTIVE?

IT'S A GROUP THAT MAKES ART OR ENGAGES IN OTHER ARTISTIC ACTIVITIES WITH A CERTAIN IDEOLOGY OR PHILOSOPHY.

THIS IS ONE OF THOSE GROUPS.

アートノススメ
Art Picks

"NO MARKs."

CREAK

YOU THINK CHANGING HOW WE INTERACT WITH OUR NEIGHBORS WOULD HELP?

I'M KIRIO FUJI, THE LEADER OF "NO MARKS."

WOULD YOU MIND TELLING ME YOUR NAME?

HELLO.

ANYONE SEE MY COPY OF *DOMU* AROUND?

...SHE NEVER USES IT.

EVEN WHEN THERE'S FANCY SHAMPOO FOR HER TO USE...

SHE JUST TELLS ME, "THE SCRUBBER AND SOAP ARE MORE THAN ENOUGH."

IT WAS TERRIBLE.

DID YOU SEE AMO NEKO-YASHIKI'S EXHIBITION?

WOW. SOUNDS LIKE HER.

OH, NO! I WASN'T THINKING THAT AT ALL...

ARE YOU WONDERING IF THIS IS SOME KINDA MLM SCHEME OR NEW CULT?

SEEMS LIKE A LOT OF PEOPLE MISTAKE US FOR THOSE THINGS.

CHATTER

CHATTER

CHATTER

A room-share...?

Is this some kinda MLM...?

Are they college students...?

A cult...?

HRM もん...

HRM もん...

HRM もん...

CREAK

AH, THAT'S TOO BAD.

OH... YEAH, I CAN SEE THAT.

STROKE 51

STRAY 2.0: STUDENT EDITION

STROKE 50 END

I'M SARA KISARAGI FROM DESIGN!

AND I'M TOSHIO HISAYAMA FROM INTER-MEDIA ART.

HEY, YATORA-KUN, ARE YOU FREE TODAY?

WE'RE IN NEED OF ANOTHER GUY TO HELP US, SINCE WE HAD ONE CANCEL ON US LAST MINUTE...

WELL, TODAY, (I WAS THINKING I'D GO HOME AND WATCH MAGENDER, BUT OTHER THAN THAT) I'M FREE.

SORRY IF THIS IS SUDDEN, YAGUCHI-KUN, BUT ARE YOU BUSY TODAY?

OKAY...?

WHAT ARE WE DOING?

WELL *THAT* WAS AN ODDLY LONG PAUSE.

HUH?

YOU'RE NOT COMING, YAMATO-SAN?!

WHAAAT?

AM I SUPPOSED TO FEEL A LITTLE DOWN ABOUT THAT? I SHOULD, RIGHT?

THE RHINOCEROS BEETLE YOU'VE BEEN RAISING'S IN CRITICAL CONDITION...?

I FOUND ONE—AND IT WAS SUPER EASY!

HUH?

OH! I SPOKE TO THEM WITH KUWANA-SAN THE OTHER DAY.

She's loud.

NO, I GET IT. YOUR BEETLE COMES FIRST.

IT'S FINE, REALLY.

BUT...

IT'S NOT THAT EASY TO FIND ANOTHER GUY TO...

BOW...

...

OH MAN...

Lecture Hall 1

BACK AT MY REVIEW...

...I WAS TOTALLY UNAFFECTED.

AND BESIDES, IT WOULDN'T HAVE BEEN RIGHT FOR ME TO SAY, "WHY DON'T YOU GET ME?"

...THAT PROCESS WAS EXACTLY WHAT I NEEDED AT THE TIME.

HOW-EVER...

I UNDER-STAND WHAT PROFESSOR INUKAI IS TALKING ABOUT, TOO.

WOOOOAH

I'M STILL BROKE, SO FORGIVE ME FOR ONLY GIVING YOU THAT.

WELL, I FIGURED YOU'D SAY THAT.

WHAT? FOR REAL?!

IF YA WANNA THANK ME, DO IT WITH FOOD.

THERE YOU ARE.

ALL RIGHT, I'LL SEE YA.

I've got class.

TOSS

...

FOOD YOU GET FROM OTHERS IS THE STRONGEST!

Mm-mmm!

Gimme a bite, huh? Just a bite.

YOU'RE SO LUCKY, YAKUMO!

...YOU KNOW, YATORA-KUN...

...FOR SOME REASON, YOU'RE LOOKING MORE LIKE AN ADULT NOW.

NEEDLESS TO SAY, *GUILT* IS A FEELING THAT MAKES YOU AWARE OF SOMETHING YOU'VE DONE WRONG.

KILLING A PERSON... EATING SNACKS WHEN YOU'RE ON A DIET...

YOU BECOME AWARE OF YOUR WRONGDOING WHEN YOUR ACTIONS ARE IN OPPOSITION TO WHAT YOU *SHOULD* DO.

...

YOU COULD SAY THAT *GUILT* IS A FORM OF SELF-AWARENESS THAT IS MUCH MORE COMPLICATED THAN *ANGER* OR *SADNESS*.

AND WITH THAT...

REVIEWS WILL BE IN TWO MONTHS.

AND THERE WILL CONTINUE TO BE NO RESTRICTIONS ON MATERIALS OR SUPPLIES.

BUT *GUILT* IS ALSO A FEELING THAT CAN BE USED TO CONTROL OTHERS BY LINKING IT TO *RESPONSIBILITY*.

YOU CAN ALSO IMPROVE A SITUATION BY TURNING *GUILT* INTO AN OPPORTUNITY FOR *REFLECTION*.

THAT ASSIGNMENT HIT US LIKE A STORM...

Wow! That's the first time I've ever made it through reviews on time. You lot are too leisurely about it...

IT IS.

IS THE NEXT ONE THE LAST?

THANK YOU VERY MUCH.

Self-portrait

Tsukinoki-sensei

EACH PROFESSOR HAS THEIR OWN QUIRKS WHEN IT COMES TO ASSIGNMENTS.

WON'T IT?

MAYBE THE NEXT ONE WILL COME FROM CHOYA-SENSEI?

I DON'T WANNA DO THAT EVER AGAIN.

HAAAH

Landscape of Tokyo

Nekoyashiki-sensei

THE ONE WE JUST DID FOR INUKAI-SENSEI WAS ALL ABOUT STAMINA.

AS FOR THE DETAILS OF THAT ASSIGN-MENT...

He heard us...

...THE NEXT ASSIGN-MENT WILL ALSO BE FROM ME.

I'M SORRY TO DISAPPOINT YOU, BUT...

SO THE NEXT ASSIGN-MENT WILL...

HOW LONG...

...WILL YOU KEEP DOING THE SAME THING?

I RECALL YOU SAYING THAT YOUR YEAR-END PIECE WAS *SOMETHING YOU MADE TO FEEL SATISFIED WITH YOUR-SELF.*

WELL, THESE CROQUIS DRAWINGS LED ME TO DISCOVER SOMETHING WITHIN MYSELF AFTER AN ENTIRE YEAR OF FEELING SLUGGISH...

YOUR PIECE FOR THE FIRST-YEAR FINAL SHOW...

HUH ?

...WAS A SMALL-SCALE AUTOBIO-GRAPHICAL PIECE.

YOU DESCRIBED YOUR PERSONAL REALITY, AND AS A PICTURE, IT EVEN HAD A SIMPLE NICENESS TO IT.

WHAT AN ADRENALINE RUSH...

SERIOUSLY, JUST DIVING INTO IT AND LETTING MY HANDS DO ALL THE WORK IS TOO MUCH FUN...!

...THEY'RE IMPORTANT TO ME, AS SOMEONE WHO SPENT A YEAR NOT BEING ABLE TO SIT DOWN AND GET MY HANDS MOVING...

TELL ME...

I WOULD NEVER HAVE FINISHED IF I HADN'T TALKED TO YAKUMO-SAN. SERIOUSLY...

SHF

NEEEXT!

BUT...

THESE DRAWINGS MIGHT LOOK LIKE REGULAR CROQUIS TO OTHER PEOPLE.

STROKE 50
ONE OF THOSE SITUATIONS WHERE
I TOOK THE HEAT AND KEPT MY COOL

500 DRAW-INGS...

WITH THAT MANY DRAWINGS, IT'S IMPOSSIBLE TO START BY THINKING THINGS THROUGH BEFORE PUTTING PENCIL TO PAPER.

IT JUST DOESN'T WORK THAT WAY.

ART: TAMANA MOTEKI

SOMEHOW, WHEN I'M DRAWING...

...NO, MAYBE THAT'S NOT WHAT THIS IS.

...MY MIND IS MORE ACTIVE.

IT'S MORE LIKE...

...MY BRAIN IS ATTACHED TO MY HAND.

OH MAN, THIS PERSON LOOKS REALLY COOL WITH THIS POSE.

ON THE OTHER HAND, OLDER FOLKS DON'T SEEM TO NOTICE AT ALL— ESPECIALLY OLDER MEN...

I'LL HAVE TO BE MORE AWARE OF THE WHOLE FIGURE FOR THE NEXT ONE...

OH, I DIDN'T GET HIS FEET ON THE PAGE...

...WAIT.

ART: TAMANA MOTEKI

NO, REALLY. I WONDER IF THIS IS OKAY.

BUT IF THIS ISN'T GOOD ENOUGH, I CAN JUST DO 1,000 OF THESE.

IS THIS ENOUGH ...?

KTNK

KTHNK

I GUESS MY CONCEPT WILL HAVE TO BE SOMETHING LIKE "YOU CAN MAKE DISCOVERIES BY OBSERVING PEOPLE." THAT'LL DO.

I JUST HAVE TO DRAW... SO I'LL GO AHEAD AND DRAW PEOPLE...

...BUT THIS IS STILL THE SAME AS JUMPING THE GUN.

KTNK

KTNK

I...I FEEL LIKE I GOT PUSHED INTO DOING THIS...

...AH, CRAP, OUR EYES MET.

YOUNG PEOPLE ARE PRETTY SENSITIVE TO OTHER PEOPLE'S GAZE, HUH. THEY NOTICE ME IMMEDIATELY...

...FIRST, I'LL DRAW FULL FIGURES.

...THEN IT'S NO WONDER THAT I'VE GOTTEN WORSE.

BECAUSE I HAVEN'T BEEN MAKING ART.

FOR NOW...

BUT IT IS WHAT IT IS.

HEY!

...500 DRAW-INGS.

...SO I CAN MAKE...

I HAVE TO THINK OF SOME-THING...

UHH... PLEASE STOP. THIS IS EMBARRASSING...

OOBA-SENSEI STILL TALKS ABOUT IT IN SCHOOL!

AH HA HA HA HA HA HA HA HA HA HA HA HA HA

OH...

...HUH? YOU CALLED?

OH, NO, I WAS JUST TELLING HER HOW YOU MADE A RIDICULOUS AMOUNT OF PIECES DURING THE WINTER COURSE AT PREP SCHOOL.

AND I THOUGHT... SOME GROWTH CAN ONLY COME FROM CHURNING OUT *LOTS* OF WORK.

YEAH. *THAT...*

...

OH, SORRY. I HAVE CLASS FOR FOURTH PERIOD!

OKAY! SEE YOU LATER!

IF THAT'S THE CASE...

Oh, wow.

BECAUSE I KNOW YOU WERE THE PERSON WHO PRODUCED THE MOST WHEN WE WERE AT PREP SCHOOL.

LOOKS LIKE YAKUMO-SAN IS CLOSE TO FINISHING ALREADY...

WHOA!

FWOOSH

OH, SORRY!

I'LL GO GRAB SOMETHING TO EAT...

...

...AH, YES.

THANK YOU.

THE FIRST-YEARS' YEAR-END PIECES...

TO PUT IT BLUNTLY, THEY LACKED POWER.

Y-YOU THINK SO...?

...

INDEED, I DO.

BUT I DON'T THINK IT'S ALL THEIR FAULT.

TSUKINOKI-SENSEI, ROSEI-SENSEI, AND NEKO-YASHIKI-SENSEI BEAR RESPONSIBILITY FOR THIS, TOO.

WHAT?

ER...

...

HERE ARE THE FIRST-YEAR STUDENT FILES YOU ASKED FOR.

SLIIIINK
すすすす

Haaaah... Fwooo...

GA-CLONK

PARDON THE...

YES... WHAT IS IT?

...

KNOCK KNOCK

FFFH...

...IS A WARM-UP.

WHA?

I'm doing it?

...GO AHEAD, YUMESAKI-SAN.

I FEEL JUST AS NERVOUS KNOCKING ON THIS DOOR NOW AS I DID WHEN I WAS A STUDENT...

IF IT DOESN'T HAPPEN IN THAT ORDER, THERE WILL BE TROUBLE.

SLIIINK
すすす

"KNOCK TWICE."

"YES. COME IN."

"KA-CHAK."

Trouble how? IS INUKAI-SENSEI SOME SORTA URBAN LEGEND?

HAAH...

TO "DRAW" *DOES* MEAN SOMETHING LIKE "TO MAKE A PICTURE WITH LINES," BUT IN FINE ART, IT'S ALL RIGHT TO USE COLOR.

I was really bad at that stuff in Saeki-sensei's art class...

IT'S AMAZING HOW YAKUMO JUST KNOWS THESE THINGS. I CAN'T BELIEVE HE CLEARLY ANSWERED THAT QUESTION SO CASUALLY.

AHH, I SEE...

...

Ohh, okay.

OUT OF THOSE FIVE METHODS, *DRAWING* IS THE ONE THAT'S THE MOST *SELF-CENTERED.*

IF IT *FEELS* RIGHT, WHY *NOT* MAKE A CROQUIS-LIKE PICTURE, OR EVEN A STUDY-LIKE PICTURE?

International Travel Feature

Co-Op Student Travel!!

Limited time offer!

Special price!!

7 days

WHAT I'M SAYING IS THAT THIS ASSIGN-MENT...

IF YOU CAN PULL IT OFF! YOU COULD SPEND A LIFETIME MAKING 500 STUDIES AND STILL NEVER FINISH!

SO ARE YA SAYIN' *ANYTHING* GOES?

Inukai's Off

THIS TIME, NO ONE'S TOLD US WHAT ART MATERIALS, SIZES, OR SUPPORTING MATERIALS TO USE.

We have two weeks, you know.

CROQUIS IS MOSTLY USED FOR LIVING THINGS AND FOCUSES ON *MOVEMENT* AND *CENTER OF GRAVITY.* THIS CAN ALSO BE CALLED A GESTURE DRAWING OR LINE DRAWING.

CROQUIS IS ABOUT CAPTURING YOUR SUBJECT QUICKLY AND SIMPLY. IT'S A METHOD WHERE YOU TYPICALLY DESCRIBE THINGS USING ONLY LINES.

A SKETCH IS A METHOD OF BROADLY DESCRIBING A FIGURE OR LANDSCAPE.

IN OTHER WORDS, YOU'RE CAPTURING THE *ELEMENTS* OF YOUR SUBJECT.

AN ESQUISSE, ALSO KNOWN AS A ROUGH, IS A METHOD OF DESCRIBING THE CONCEPT OR COMPOSITION FOR A FULL PIECE OR PAINTING.

IT'S BASICALLY A PREPARATORY SKETCH.

A STUDY IS A METHOD IN WHICH YOU CAPTURE AND DESCRIBE THINGS LIKE THE *TEXTURE, TONE,* AND *POSITIONAL RELATIONSHIPS* OF YOUR SUBJECT.

THE DRAWINGS WE'RE DOING FOR THIS ASSIGNMENT WOULDN'T BE ENOUGH TO BE FULL PIECES, BUT THEY'RE MORE DEVELOPED THAN ESQUISSES...

FOR THIS ASSIGNMENT, *DRAWING* IS A METHOD IN WHICH YOU INCLUDE *COMPOSITIONAL ELEMENTS,* LIKE YOU WOULD FOR ANY PIECE, WHILE ALSO PRODUCING SOMETHING FROM YOUR IMAGINATION IN A FREE AND IMPROVISED WAY.

TO BEGIN WITH...

...WHAT EXACTLY *IS* A "DRAWING," ANYWAY?

I can't Fail a course!

IF I CAN'T GET MY COURSE CREDITS UNLESS I TURN IN 500 DRAWINGS...

"TO DRAW" USUALLY MEANS TO CREATE A PICTURE WITH LINES, SO WE'RE TALKING ABOUT SOME SORT OF LINEAR EXPRESSION, RIGHT...?

SO DOES THAT MEAN WE CAN'T USE COLOR?

Now that you mention it...

YEAH, IN ARCHITECTURE, IT CAN BE SOMETHING LIKE A "DRAFT"...

YEAH, SEE WHAT I MEAN?

...THEN I CAN'T MESS UP A SINGLE DRAWING, RIGHT?! IF EVEN ONE SHEET DOESN'T FIT THE DEFINITION OF A DRAWING, IT'S OVER...

HEY YAKUMO, THIS IS GONNA GET EMBARRASSING IF YOU KEEP THIS UP. DON'T OVERDO IT.

GYA HA HA

LOOKS LIKE HE PLANS ON USING THE BACKS OF FLYERS FOR HIS ASSIGNMENT.

WHAT'S HE DOING...?

EVEN AT ONE DRAWING A DAY, IT WOULD TAKE MORE THAN A YEAR.

500 DRAWINGS, HUH...

500 DRAWINGS...

Copy paper

Copy paper 500 count ¥580

BUT WHAT KIND OF CONCEPT WORKS WITH 500 DRAWINGS ...?

AND SINCE WE'RE TURNING IT IN AS AN ASSIGNMENT, IT'S PROBABLY NOT GOING TO WORK IF I "JUST DREW" STUFF.

EVEN IF I DREW A BUNCH OF DIFFERENT THINGS, THEY WOULD HAVE TO HAVE SOME KIND OF "CONCEPT" TO STRING THEM TOGETHER...

...

IN *MY* CASE, THIS IS A DOWNER.

'CAUSE I'M BETTER AT USING MY BODY THAN MY HEAD!

YOU'RE ALL SMILES, KINEMI-CHAN.

Copy paper 500 count ¥580

I ALREADY TOLD YOU—I'M *CONSIDERING* IT! I'LL ALSO INTRODUCE YOU TO MY FRIENDS, SO I'LL NEED ANOTHER 50 SHEETS...

UM, BUT... ARE YOU REALLY GOING TO MAKE A CONTRACT WITH US...?

OH, THE BACK OF THESE ARE WHITE, TOO!

OH, THIS PAPER'S STURDIER, HUH?!

I WAS ONE STEP BEHIND...

SORRY, BUT SOME STUDENTS CAME IN BEFORE AND BOUGHT ALL OF THEM...

Counter

BUT I GUESS I'M STUCK. I'LL HAVE TO STOP BY YODOBASHI* ON THE WAY BACK...

I THOUGHT COPY PAPER WOULD BE THE CHEAPEST...

HM?

*"YODOBASHI" CAMERA, A MAJOR JAPANESE RETAIL CHAIN THAT SELLS ELECTRONICS AND PHOTO EQUIPMENT.

YOUR DEADLINE IS TWO WEEKS FROM NOW.

HOWEVER, I CAN'T HAVE YOU POSTING ALL 500 DRAWINGS ON THE WALL...

...SO YOU WILL ONLY BE DISPLAYING A PORTION OF THE 500.

I'LL ASK YOU TO LEAVE THE REST IN A STACK IN YOUR EXHIBITION SPACE.

What? Two weeks...?!

Isn't that too short?

IS THAT EVEN POSSIBLE?

500...

MRMR

IF I DO SOME QUICK MATH, THAT COMES OUT TO 16 DRAWINGS PER DAY...

500 DRAWINGS OVER 30 DAYS...

ASSIGNMENT GIVEN

FOR NEKOYASHIKI-SENSEI'S "TOKYO" ASSIGNMENT IN OUR FIRST YEAR, WE HAD A MONTH UNTIL FINAL REVIEWS.

INTER-MEDIARY REVIEWS

FINAL REVIEWS

THAT'S STILL A LOT, EVEN IF THEY'RE JUST DRAWINGS...

IN THAT CASE, THE DUE DATE SHOULD BE A LITTLE FURTHER OUT, TOO...

IF THIS ASSIGNMENT IS SCHEDULED THE SAME WAY, THEN...

AS FOR THE SCHEDULE...

THE FIRST ASSIGNMENT FOR YOUR SECOND YEAR...

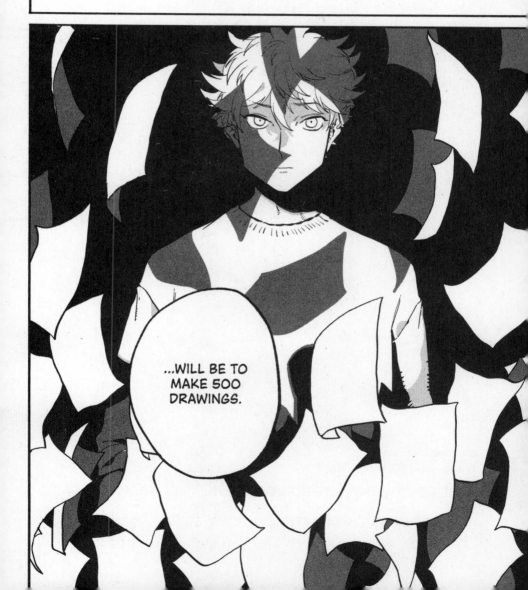

...WILL BE TO MAKE 500 DRAWINGS.

STROKE 49

WHERE'S THE WALKTHROUGH SITE THAT'LL SHOW ME
HOW TO BEAT THIS DEATHLOOP OF WORRY

THE FIRST
ASSIGNMENT
FOR YOUR
SECOND
YEAR...

...WILL BE TO
MAKE 500
DRAWINGS.

...IT MEANS THE PROBLEMS ARE WITH THE UNIVERSITY ITSELF AND THE TEACHERS, RIGHT?

ALL RIGHT ...

I REEEALLY DON'T WANT TO WORK ON ASSIGNMENTS.

...I'M NOT THE ONLY ONE HAVING A TOUGH TIME IN UNIVERSITY?

IF THAT'S THE CASE,

THEN IT'S NOT THAT THERE'S ANYTHING WRONG WITH ME...

...

I MEAN, THE REVIEWS AND THINGS CAN BE SUPER HARSH HERE, SO I GET IT.

AT THE END OF MY FIRST YEAR, SOMEONE TOLD ME, "YOU MAKE BETTER PIECES WHEN YOU'RE STRUGGLING."

OHH...

...HUH?

...BUT HONESTLY, I WANT TO GRADUATE AS SOON AS POSSIBLE.

IT TOOK A LOT JUST TO GET IN HERE...

I DON'T THINK I CAN BECOME A GOOD STUDENT.

HAAAA!

WAIT, SO DOES THAT MEAN...?

YOU SHOULD COME HANG OUT AT THE CRAFT STUDIO NEXT TIME, YAGUCHI-KUN.

OH. I GOTTA GO BUY SOME WASHI PAPER.

EVEN THOUGH WE'RE ALL ART STUDENTS...!

THIS IS THE FIRST TIME I'VE REALLY SPOKEN WITH PEOPLE NOT IN OIL PAINTING.

...EVERYONE'S DOING TOTALLY DIFFERENT THINGS.

FOR REAL?!

I'D REALLY LIKE THAT!

TWO PEOPLE IN MY DEPARTMENT QUIT LAST YEAR, AND ONE IS TAKING A BREAK FROM SCHOOL. IT'S WILD.

WOW, REALLY?

HUH? QUIT...? I DON'T THINK ANYONE HAS.

THAT REMINDS ME, HAVE ANY OF THE OIL PAINTING STUDENTS QUIT YET?

I...

...

NAH, DOESN'T MATTER.

GUESS THAT EXPLAINS WHY NEKOYASHIKI-SENSEI WAS AFRAID OF HIM...

HUH?

IT'S CLEAR WHEN YOU SEE THEM INTERACT.

IS...IS THAT TRUE?

I BET THAT GUY'S PRETTY BRUTAL.

OH.

AN ASSIGN-MENT, HUH...

ASSIGN-MENT.

ANYWAY, I WONDER WHAT KINDA ASSIGNMENT WE'RE GONNA GET FROM THAT GUY.

?

THAT GUY'S SORT OF A BIG DEAL HERE.

OH, I KNOW WHAT'CHA MEAN. HOW OLD D'YA THINK HE IS?

HE HAS A KIND OF COOL AND REFINED AIR TO HIM.

SO INUKAI-SENSEI'S OUR PROFESSOR NOW.

HE'S ONE OF THE VICE-PRESIDENTS OF TUA.

HE DOES GIVE OFF THAT VIBE.

OH, WOW.

WHA? HE IS?!

HE'S ALSO EXHIBITED AT THE LA BIENNALE DI VENEZIA IN THE PAST.

HIS WORK MAINLY CONSISTS OF PAINTINGS AND ILLUSTRATIONS.

HE'S BEEN A PROFESSOR AT THIS SCHOOL FOR CLOSE TO 20 YEARS, AND HE'S THE MOST DISTINGUISHED PERSON IN OIL PAINTING HERE.

NOW THEN...

I LOOK FORWARD TO A PLEASANT YEAR WITH YOU ALL.

UHHHM...

INUKAI-SENSEI, WHAT'RE YOU DOING?

I GUESS I JUST CAN'T COME AROUND ON THE SWEETNESS OF KETCHUP...

I *DO* LIKE TOMATOES, THOUGH.

AND I DON'T EXACTLY *HATE* PROCESSED FOODS OR ADDITIVES...

OH, UHH...

HMM.

FEEL FREE TO DO THE SAME, CHOYA-SAN.

I'M INTRO-DUCING MYSELF.

I LIKE LOW-MALT BEER.

UNTIL THEN, PLEASE REGISTER FOR YOUR CLASSES AND SO ON.

I WILL HAND YOU YOUR ASSIGNMENT PROMPTS ONE WEEK FROM NOW.

THEY CERTAINLY SEEM *ECCENTRIC*...

Yup.

MY FAVORITE FOOD...

...IS RAW MEAT.

AND MY LEAST FAVORITE FOOD...

...IS KETCHUP SPAGHETTI.

I'M NOT FOND OF KETCHUP.

ER...

...

YEAH...

WELL, Y'KNOW... I, UH, WAS WORRIED YOU GUYS MIGHT SLACK OFF N' STUFF...

AND I HAD NOTHIN' ELSE TO DO, SINCE I'M NOT ASSIGNED TO A SPECIFIC YEAR!

OKAY, MOM!

There's no way you had nothing else to do...

YAKUMO-SAN?

NOW THEN...

AND I'LL BE OVERSEEING THAT ASSIGNMENT.

ONE WEEK FROM NOW, YOU WILL ALL RECEIVE AN ASSIGNMENT.

...!

BY THE WAY...

NEKOYASHIKI-SENSEI IS UNDERTAKING A BIG PROJECT THIS YEAR.

YES.

AND TSUKINOKI-SENSEI HAS BEEN HAVING BACK PROBLEMS, SO THEY WILL BOTH BE STEPPING AWAY FROM THEIR TEACHING DUTIES THIS YEAR.

AND I'M HIS ASSISTANT, SAKURAI. I LOOK FORWARD TO A GOOD YEAR WITH YOU ALL.

ROSEI-SENSEI WILL CONTINUE TO TEACH THIS COHORT.

...

THAT SAID, WE STILL PLAN FOR YOU TO HAVE OPPORTUNITIES TO SPEAK WITH PROFESSORS BESIDES US.

WAIT. YUMESAKI-SAN, WEREN'T YOU NEKOYASHIKI-SENSEI'S ASSISTANT...?

...I'M GONNA MISS THEM A LITTLE.

YEAH...

A-AND...

I-I'M...

SHIBATA...

OH, SHIT...

PROF. INUKAI ...!

IT'S A PLEASURE TO MEET YOU ALL.

SO...

SO THESE NEW TEACHERS ARE REPLACING TSUKINOKI-SENSEI AND NEKOYASHIKI-SENSEI!?

AND I'M HIS ASSISTANT, ARIMURA! NICE TO MEET YOUUUU!

JEEZ, INUKAI-SENSEI'S A TOUGH ACT TO FOLLOW...

I'LL ALSO BE TEACHING THE SECOND YEARS THIS TIME AROUND. NAME'S CHOYA.

...THE PEOPLE HANDLING YOUR COHORT THIS YEAR ARE CHANGING, APART FROM US THREE.

GREET-INGS.

Oh, excuse me...

HUH?

GOOD MORNING, EVERYONE.

...TO BEGIN THE FIRST MEETING OF YOUR SECOND YEAR.

IT'S TIME...

NO.

THERE ARE FOUR MORE PEOPLE COMING— THE OTHER PROFESSORS AND THEIR ASSISTANTS.

HOW-EVER...

WAIT. ARE THERE ONLY THREE OF YOU?

...

THEY TAKE THICK-CUT FRIED TOFU AND BEAN SPROUTS, STIR-FRY THEM IN BUTTER AND SOY SAUCE, AND PLACE IT OVER A BOWL OF RICE!

OMF もぐ

BUTTER-DON?

NOMF もぐ

YEAH, IT'S TUA'S SPECIALTY RICE BOWL.

OMF もぐ NOMF もぐ

OMF もぐ

IT'S SOMETHING THEY USED TO SERVE REGULARLY BACK IN THE DAY, BUT THEY BROUGHT IT BACK FOR A LIMITED TIME ONLY.

WHY DON'T YOU GIVE IT A TRY, YAGUCHI?

I'm gonna buy one, too.

LOOKS LIKE A PRETTY HARDY MEAL.

WE'RE EATING IT BEFORE OUR CLASS MEETINGS TO FUEL UP!

ごくっ
GULP?

...THANK-FULLY, YES.

AND YOU PASSED THE EXAMS?

WOW, AWE-SOME!!!

AW, COME ON! IT'S NOT LIKE I WAS HIDING IT FROM ANYONE.

WELL, I DID ATTEND A HIGH SCHOOL FOR THE ARTS, Y'KNOW.

IN FACT, SCULPTURE HAS BEEN A LOT OF FUN,

AND I'VE EVEN DISCOVERED SOME THINGS ABOUT PAINTING WHILE TRYING MY HAND AT SCULPTURE.

I ACTUALLY TRANSFERRED INTO THE SCULPTURE COURSE AT TAI AROUND MAY LAST YEAR...

I DIDN'T END UP GOING WITH OIL PAINTING...

...BUT BACK THEN...

NO...

THANKS FOR BEFORE— FOR WHAT YOU SAID WHEN WE RAN INTO EACH OTHER AT THE ZOO.

SO, LIKE...

AND TODAY IS THE FIRST DAY...

BEEN A WHILE...

...I WORKED PART-TIME FOR THREE MONTHS AT A COMMUNITY ART SCHOOL.

AFTER FINISHING MY FIRST YEAR OF UNIVERSITY...

...OF MY SECOND YEAR AS A UNIVERSITY STUDENT.

...YAGUCHI-SENPAI!

STROKE 48 MY LEAST FAVORITE FOOD IS KETCHUP SPAGHETTI

CHARACTERS

Yotasuke Takahashi

After quitting the prep school that he and Yatora had been attending, he studied on his own and passed TUA's exams on his first attempt. His talent, skills, and unsociable character inspire Yatora to be a better artist.

Maki Kuwana

A former prep-school classmate of Yatora's. She failed her entrance exams but is still striving to get into an art school. She's been studying sculpture at prep school, but...

Yatora Yaguchi

After getting hooked on the joy of making art, he studied to get into Tokyo University of the Arts, the most competitive of all Japanese art colleges, and passed on his first attempt. He's a hardworking normie.

Yakumo Murai

An all-around knowledgeable guy who is constantly redefining what it means to be "the strongest." He's taken a liking to Yatora.

Haruka Hashida

He used to attend the same prep school as Yatora. He's currently attending Tama Art University.

TABLE OF CONTENTS

BLUE PERIOD 12

TSUBASA YAMAGUCHI

Some artists produce work while living together